THE RELATIONS OF HIGHER EDUCATION TO NATIONAL PROSPERITY.

AN

ORATION

DELIVERED BEFORE THE

PHI BETA KAPPA SOCIETY

OF THE

UNIVERSITY OF VERMONT,

JUNE 27, 1876.

By CHARLES KENDALL ADAMS,
Professor of History in the University of Michigan.

PUBLISHED BY THE SOCIETY.

BURLINGTON:
FREE PRESS PRINT.
1876.

ORATION.

Mr. President ; Brothers in Phi Beta Kappa:

I purpose to speak to you to-day on the Relations of Higher Education to National Prosperity. I deem this subject appropriate to the season and the occasion, inasmuch as at the present time, as perhaps never before, thoughtful men and women are reviewing the history of our nation, and scrutinizing with somewhat more than usual care the foundations on which our governmental structure has been reared. It is fitting, moreover, that on such an anniversary as this we should look to the future as well as to the past. It is as true as it is commonplace to say that in a few years the country with all its precious interests will be in the hands of those who are now leaving the schools. There is constantly going on a silent revolution which is taking the political power out of the hands of those who held it yesterday, and placing it in the hands of those who are to wield it to-morrow. In scarcely more than a score of years, all those who are now in active life will have been gently crowded from the scene and a new generation will have taken their places. This mighty change, ever going on, like one of the great processes of nature, "silently, effectually, inevitably," is rolling the accumulated weight of all the knowledge and civilization of the world upon the rising generation, asking it to carry it on a little way, and then to hand it over to its successors. It is not yet half a generation since the outbreak of the great civil war, and yet the men who then controlled public opinion are passed away. Lincoln and Douglas, Seward and Stanton, Breckenridge and Sumner, Stevens and

Greeley are all gone. He whom the people have twice placed gratefully at the head of the nation, was then struggling for a precarious existence in a western city, and the best of the present governors in the South was then a student in college. The honored and the powerful of to-day were then the obscure and the unknown.

But interesting as this silent revolution is of itself, its real importance springs from another cause. It comes rather from the momentous fact that, while we inherit the political duties and responsibilities of our fathers, we cannot inherit their skill and their knowledge. It is doubtless a benign, as it certainly is an impressive, provision of divine economy, that learning and skill cannot be transmitted from father to son. We may inherit intellectual appetites, but not intellectual possessions. All the knowledge, the art, the refinement in existence, must either be acquired by those who are assuming the active duties of life, or must perish with those who are putting off those duties, and be lost forever.

It is for these reasons that in every civilized community the cause of education is a subject of momentous importance. It is for these reasons that it is impossible to preserve—not to say to augment—the general stock of intelligence without large and increasing expenditures for the education of the young. It is for these reasons that, the moment the zeal of the public in this direction begins to flag, the average intelligence of the community begins to decline.

In our own country the cause of elementary education has flourished as almost nowhere else in the world. Combined influences have contributed to this result. The cause has had many and eloquent advocates. Horace Mann, devoting the rare powers of his mind, the indomitable energy of his character, and the best years of his life to his favorite work; Edward Everett, pleading eloquently "The Importance of Education in a Republic," are but representatives of a great host of distinguished men who are entitled to the gratitude of the nation. And the nation honors them. Till the Republic is forgotten, they will be revered as among its greatest benefactors.

Then in accord with this advocacy, has been the influence of our material prosperity. Every intelligent lad sees something of the glittering prizes that are offered to industrious effort. Fortunes rapidly accumulated have displayed, in our own country as nowhere else, their alluring and often irresistible charms. The professions, seemingly over crowded, and yet never full, keep up an importunate voice of appeal alike to the ambitious and the indolent.

Now the result of these apparently diverse influences upon society has been precisely what *a priori* might have been anticipated. The voice of our educators has been simply reinforced by the voice of our materialism in demanding a thorough and comprehensive system of common school education. There is not a boy, there is not a laborer with a spark of parental desire for the prosperity of his child, who does not see that at least a common school education is the first condition of an ability to profit by the opportunities of life.

But as soon as we pass beyond the domain of instruction purely elementary, we find that these two forces no longer act in harmony. The calls of ambition are now, not toward the schools, but toward the forum and the market; and consequently, whether these voices are simply discordant, or whether the voice of the educators is drowned and silenced amid the hoarse jargon of affairs, the result is the same, —that while our common schools flourish and are the just pride of our country, our higher institutions of learning have been left, for the most part, either to perish, or to subsist upon the precarious favors of private benevolence.

I am not so unjust as to attribute what seems to me to have been the languishing condition of American colleges during the past twenty-five years exclusively to the cause which I have assigned. There is, as it seems to me, another cause, and possibly one that is still more important. I refer to the fact that a more or less radical change had taken place in public opinion concerning the relations of higher education to the state at large. It was the doctrine of the Puritan fathers—and it is of great importance to note the fact—a doctrine continued for a hundred and fifty years, through all the dark periods of our colonial and provincial history, that the encouragement of higher education was one of the great interests of the state. It was no doctrine of theirs, that the colleges were not, equally with the lower schools, entitled to the fostering care of the commonwealth. It seems never to have entered their imaginations, that university education, less than common school education, was the interest of the entire people. Two years before John Harvard gave his name together with half of his estate and the whole of his library to the college at Cambridge, the General Court of Massachusetts had voted for the same purpose a sum equal to "a years rate of the whole colony." President Quincy, in his History of Harvard University, declares that during the whole of the first seventy years of its existence, "its officers were dependent for daily bread upon the bounty of the General Court." Eloquent praises have been bestowed, and doubtless justly bestowed, upon the noble generosity of individual colonists for their sacrifices in order to establish "for learning, a resting place, and for science, a fixed habitation on the borders of the wilderness;" but it ought not to be forgotten that this noble generosity was but the smallest source of income to the University. It was to the more substantial gifts of the Legislature, that the prosperity of the college was chiefly due. Nor did this dependence upon the General Court cease with the colonial days of Massachusetts. When a State constitution came to be adopted, that instrument devoted one entire chapter to the interests of the only college under its jurisdiction. "It shall be the duty," so runs the constitution, "it shall be the duty of all legislatures and magistrates, in all future periods of this commonwealth, to cherish the interests of literature and science, and all seminaries of them, especially the University at Cambridge, public schools and grammar schools in the towns." Thus it will be seen that Massachusetts considered the University as preeminently a part of her school system.

The history of Yale is, in this respect, not unlike that of Harvard. President Dwight, in his sketch of the college, assures us that "the beginning of this seminary" was at the General Court, held at Guilford in June of 1652. At that time it was decided after a full consideration of the question, that New England could not support two colleges, and, therefore, in order that they might not, by founding a new college, embarrass Harvard, the matter was indefinitely postponed. It was not until fifty years later that the college was actually founded. The same high authority which I have already quoted says, "the princ pal benefactor, both during this period and all which have succeeded, was the Legislature." In illustration of the method pursued it may be said that the General Court in its first charter provided for an annual grant to the college—a grant which was continued until 1755. In 1750 Connecticut Hall was reared from money chiefly contributed by the Legislature. In 1792 the Legislature granted money with which four new buildings were erected, a handsome addition was made to the library, "a complete philosophical and chemical apparatus was procured," and finally, three new professorships were established. Thus down to the beginning of the present century Yale, no less than Harvard, was chiefly indebted to the State Legislature for the means of its prosperity and its advancement.

Nor was this method of supporting the higher schools of learning confined to New England. The college of William and Mary, in the order of its establishment second only to Harvard, was founded by an endowment from the royal domain, and was supported, for the most part, by the income of "a tax of a penny a pound on tobacco exported to other plantations." In Maryland, South Carolina and Georgia, the same provident care of the colleges by the State was inaugurated. And if in those states the cause of higher education was less prosperous than at the North, the fact was largely, if not chiefly, due to the earlier adoption of that policy of the multiplication of colleges which in the present century has spread over the whole country. Maryland, as early as 1723, provided for High Schools in all the counties of the State. The early efforts of the State in the cause of education, as President Sparks has said, were "liberal, honorable, and worthy of the highest praise." But the Legislature made one fatal mistake. Instead of concentrating its resources on a single college or university, it divided its means, and raised three of its high schools to the rank of colleges. Jealousies ensued. In the course of a few years, it came to be seen that schools which, as academies, had been admirable, as colleges, were insignificant. So universal, indeed, became the dissatisfaction, that in 1805 the State withdrew it said altogether; and thus, notwithstanding the munificent efforts of the State in its early history, its colleges at the beginning of the present century had dwindled into abject feebleness.

In South Carolina, a wiser course was pursued, and, therefore, the cause of higher education escaped, though it *barely* escaped, the fate which befell it in Maryland. Although the State committed the error of establishing four colleges where but a single one could be supported, the nature of the mistake came to be seen and the proper remedy was applied. In 1801 the Legislature established the College of South Carolina on so liberal a basis that the other colleges at once descended to the rank of preparatory schools. Within a few years the State gave to the college at Columbia some $300 000, an amount which at the beginning of this century was truly magnificent. But no state ever made a better investment. During the first half of the present century the scholastic accomplishments and the political ability of the statesmen of South Carolina were the just pride of the State, as they would have been of any State.

Thus, wherever we look, whether among the Puritans of New England, the Catholics of Maryland, or the Episcopalians of Virginia and South Carolina, we everywhere, down to the beginning of this century, behold the same general educational conditions, the same general habit of supporting the higher schools as well as the lower at the expense of the state.

It is moreover interesting to note that it was in schools thus endowed and thus supported that the master minds which framed this republic were developed. If, as we go to the "Mecca of this patriotic year," we see reason to rejoice in a national greatness or a national prosperity, it is because of the spirit and the wisdom of the men who were trained in schools thus established and thus endowed. It was from inspiration gained from such sources that Thomas Jefferson, the man whom Lord Brougham pronounced the greatest champion of the political rights and interests of the common people that ever lived, could write in 1800, the very year of his election to the Presidency, and at the age of fifty-five, those words to Dr. Priestley, which can never fail to be a delight to every classical scholar who reads them:—"I enjoy Homer in his own language infinitely better than Pope's translation of him. I thank on my knees Him who directed my early education, for having put into my possession this rich source of delight; and I would not exchange it for anything which I could then have acquired, and have not since acquired."

But we have now to note that as time advanced, new elements arose to complicate the educational problem. Local demands and local jealousies began to find expression, and ere long came to be importunate, if not indeed imperious. A still more potent influence was the fact that the various religious denominations, as they came to be spread over the country, felt the need of educational support. They understood well that whether or not a state can thrive without educated statesmen, no religious denomination can push its way in the nineteenth century without an educated clergy. Accordingly, in the course of half a century, colleges, for these combined reasons, were planted by the score in localities where no more than a single one could be adequately supported.

Now it is of the first importance to note the immediate effect of this policy, which was nothing less than to paralyze all efforts to secure appropriations for higher education from the state legislatures. The reasoning which led to this paralysis was of the simplest nature possible. The state could not support all, and, therefore no course was open, but for it to withdraw its support altogether, and to turn over the interests of the colleges to the various religious denominations and to the localities in whose interest they had been individually established. Then began the system of private appeal; or rather, I should say, the system of private appeal already inaugurated in the numerous new colleges, came to be universally adopted in those that had already acquired renown State support was now either withdrawn altogether, or was meted out with a sparing hand.

Then, a second consequence followed hard upon the first, —indeed sprang directly out of the first. The fierce competition for students of such a superfluity of colleges kept down the educational standard; and often the still fiercer struggle for life made it necessary that the best talent of the college, as one of the victims of the system once sadly but somewhat facetiously described it, should be devoted to the work of exhorting the brethren and of expectantly waiting at the death-bed of the childless and the widow. Such a system could not but be productive of deplorable results. It was impossible for men, however scholarly and learned they might be,—and many of them were scholarly and learned,—to beget and disseminate in the community either a high respect for collegiate honors or an ardent desire to obtain them.

It is perhaps worthy of note, in passing, that it was at this stage of our educational progress, that the discovery was made that it is unsafe to send young men to institutions receiving the patronage of the state. As we have already seen, the Episcopalians of Virginia, the Catholics of Maryland, and even the stern Puritans of New England, did not imagine for more than a hundred and fifty years that there was any dividing line between the methods by which the lower schools and the higher were to be supported. But now for the first time, the doctrine came to be entertained, that the youth of the land would be in danger in any other schools than in those directly or indirectly under the control of the churches. Fond parents who did not scruple to commit their tender and impressible children to the uncertain influences of unknown teachers and unknown schoolmates in the common schools, now strangely discovered, that, as soon as the child emerges from the impressible age and begins to assert an independence of thought and action, to send him to any other than a distinctively religious school, would be, at least, to imperil his faith and to jeopard his morals.

Such, as it seems to me, are some of the influences that have been at work to embarrass and enfeeble the cause of higher education. I endeavor to present nothing more than the plainest picture in the plainest possible colors. If any one suspects that I have overdrawn it, I ask him candidly to look at the result. I ask him,—if he is familiar with what a great university ought to be and is,—to look over the magnificent array of States admitted to the Union since the Revolutionary war, and tell me how many colleges and universities there are that can be called worthy of the wealth and the enterprise and the general intelligence of this country. And if some one replies that time is necessary to develop our system, I answer that the Universities of Bonn and Munich and Berlin have all been founded since the beginning of this century, and that not one of them had been in existence a score of years before it had acquired world-wide renown through the labors of its teachers and scholars. It is a fact, I think, of the greatest significance to us Americans, that Niebuhr the father of modern history, and Liebig the founder of organic chemistry, and Hegel the author of the most influential school of modern philosophy, all acquired their imperishable renown in universities less than a quarter of a century old. The youngest of the German universities, with the exception of the one founded in the territory acquired in the war of 1870, will this very year celebrate the semi-centennial anniversary of its organization, and can boast of some two hundred professors and scarcely less than two thousand students. This is the answer to the declaration that our colleges must be venerable before they can be great.

But it is time to enquire what has been the influence of our so-called "system of higher education," upon the real educational condition of the country. What has been done in the way of encouraging young men to seek a collegiate education by this long array of two hundred and eighty-five colleges and universities, all of them entitled, so far as municipal law can bestow it, to the right of ranking themselves as schools of the highest learning? We are not left in doubt as to what the answer of this question must be.

It would be easy to show *a priori* that this undue multiplication of colleges would diminish the esteem in which colleges and universities are held. But we are not left to the unsatisfactory conclusions of *a priori* reasoning. Statistics have been accumulated which show conclusively what the tendency has been in different portions of the country. And what is this tendency? It is that, ever since the earliest period for which statistics have been preserved, the proportionate number of students seeking a collegiate education has steadily diminished. Nor is this diminution confined to any single portion of the country. In New England as a whole, for example, the proportion of students in college in 1826 was one in 1513; in 1855 it was only one in 1689; in 1869 the ratio had declined so that there were only at the rate of one in 1927. In the country as a whole, according to the carefully prepared statistics of President Barnard, the number of students in college in proportion to the population was, in 1840, one in 1549; in 1860, one in 2012; in 1869, one in 2546.

Thus it is obvious that the number of undergraduate students for thirty or forty years previous to 1870 was in our country not only diminishing, but that the diminution during the last ten years of the period, was especially remarkable. In all parts of the country, the sad fact stares us in the face that the training which has long been considered essential to finished scholarship has been losing ground from year to year in the favor of the people.

Now to this result it is probable that a number of causes have contributed. The prevailing mercenary spirit has doubtless exerted an influence. It is possible, moreover, that something has been lost from the fact that courses of study have not conformed to the public demand. But there is another cause which is probably far more important than these. It is the fact that the modern college has lost something of its former significance in the popular imagination. Ambitious young men who aspire to professional and political honors are not less numerous than were the same class fifty years ago. We cannot but believe that these young men would resort to the same means of helping themselves forward, if those means were to present to their ambition the same attractions. But the same attractions do not exist. A single one of our Western States has no less than nine universities and thirty-three colleges. Forty-two universities and colleges in a single state are not only sure to *be* insignificant, but, what is only less unfortunate, are sure to be *thought* insignificant. When the popular imagination attaches to the college but little importance, the ambitious youth is likely to eschew the college, and betake himself at once to the more attractive experience of the bar and the political arena.

Now this is not a mere picture of the fancy; it is a representation which is seen from such statistics as have been accumulated to be absolutely true to the life. In the professions (with the possible exception of the clerical) and in positions of high political trust, the proportion of college bred men is considerably less than it was in the early years of this century. Of the signers of the Declaration, thirty out of fifty-six were college bred. Of the Senate of the First Congress, fifteen out of twenty-six; while of the Forty-first Congress, the latest of which information is accessible, the proportion was only seven out of twenty-six. If the investigation were to be carried to the House of Representatives, the proportion would probably be still more unfavorable. It is thus obvious that college graduates are politically less conspicuous than they were formerly, just as we have seen them to be less numerous.

But there is another question to be asked. If, under the system which has prevailed, the number of students going to college has diminished, what has been the effect of the system on the scholarship of those who graduate? On this point it is of course difficult to speak with positive assurance. But this may be said. The same public opinion which tends by its indifference to prevent boys from going to college will at least be easily reconciled to a low standard of scholarship. Moreover it must be remembered that where indifference concerning high scholarship prevails, the fierce competition of small colleges must tend to depress rather than to elevate the standard. The struggle is often a struggle for life, and life too frequently depends not so much upon scholarship, as upon scholars.

Every educator is aware that the greatest obstacle in the way of elevating the standard of scholarship is the difficulty of raising the preparatory schools; and this difficulty arises very largely, if not chiefly, from the fact that the necessities of the smaller colleges require them to accept of whatever preparation comes to their hand. If in those states which have a college in almost every county, the condition of the colleges is deplorable, the condition of the preparatory schools is scarcely better. Hence it is that, whenever the standard of scholarship is raised, it has to be done both in reliance upon the exceptional excellence of a few tried schools, and in expectation that the size of the classes in college will be materially diminished. No college or university can prosper unless it is in some sense *en rapport* with the preparatory schools, and therefore it is that the work of raising the standard of scholarship is both slow and difficult, —little less than the fabled work of Sisyphus:—

> * * adverso nixantem trudere monte
> Saxum.

But notwithstanding all these facts, interesting and significant as they are of themselves, the most important question has not yet been reached. The question of transcendent importance is this: What has been the effect of our system upon the standards of attainment held up before the public? Are our professional men *better* fitted, or *worse* fitted, for their work than were men of the same class fifty years ago? Are our *mechanics* better, or are they worse? Are our *statesmen* and *politicians* men of broader culture, of more comprehensive views and of greater integrity; or are they inferior to the same class of men of a hundred years ago?

Now I would not answer these questions of so vital importance in any pessimistic spirit. I desire to avoid exaggeration; and I concede that there is always a tendency to disparage the present in comparison with the past. I remember that Hesiod deplored the degeneracy of his own age and sang the glories of the days of his fathers. The Sophists of Greece were little but an organized body of quacks and complainers of the condition of their own time. Cicero mourned over the degenerate poetry of Bavius and Mævius; and the critics and grammarians of Alexandria in ridiculing the men of their time only succeeded in setting up "a kingdom of learned dullness and empty profession." England in the days of Walpole was openly governed by the belief that every man had his price; and even at the beginning of the present century, seats in parliament were openly sold to the highest bidder. I admit then, without reserve, that there have always been corrupt men in politics, and pretenders in literature and science. Greece had her Alcibiades, Rome had her Verres, and even our own revolutionary age had its Arnold and its Aaron Burr. All this I concede. I admit that no age has been exempt from the affliction of pretense and dishonesty.

Nor do I esteem it a reproach that the statesmen of to-day fall below the political stature of those who framed the constitution; for who can read the political writings of Jefferson, and Adams, and Hamilton, and Madison, and not count them as worthy to rank with the foremost men of all time,—almost indeed with those intellectual giants who, according to the figure of Machiavelli, rise far above the level of their fellow men, and, stretching out their hands to each other across the interval of the ages, transmit to succeeding generations the torch of art and poetry and political science? In these days, so redolent of sweet memories of great men and great deeds, it is no disparagement, but an exaltation rather, to be allowed to sit at their feet and acknowledge their superior virtues.

But though all these considerations have their weight, we ought not to be deterred by them from a rational examination of our own age; and after all concessions are made to that tendency of human nature of which I have spoken, I fear it will have to be admitted, that we are living in an age of low standards and of cheap fame.

Now I have no purpose to ring the mournful changes on the trite topic of political corruption and of pretentious and aspiring ignorance. It may be, as has been said, that this is not so much an age of frauds as an age of the exposure of frauds; but whether this dictum be true or not, it is certain that there is throughout the country a growing tendency among thoughtful persons to take melancholy views of our political methods and our political tendencies. In regard to this political *malaise* I shall pause only to say, that, in every age and among every people, there have been corrupt men and ignorant men, who have aspired to place and pelf; and furthermore, that always their aspirations have been ardent just in proportion to their prospects of success. If in our time, or in any time, therefore, there is especial thrift of ignorance and dishonesty, the remedy is not in merely complaining of it, but in the slow and arduous work of so changing public opinion as to make its thrift impossible. It is coming to be a practical question whether we do not often exhaust our strength in attempting to reform bad men, when we should be devoting our energies to the work of selecting and using good men.

It was a saying of Kant, that out of wood so crooked as that of which man is made nothing absolutely straight can ever be formed. The saying is but an amplification of a far higher authority, and is doubtless true. But even Kant would admit that there are degrees of crookedness and perversity, and it therefore becomes a practical question to know how far the energies of the country ought to be exerted in correcting the perversity of perverse men. Surely the master mechanic does not expend his energies in trying to straighten the crooked wood with which the forests abound; and may it not be possible —I ask the question simply as a query—may it not be possible that the present age is using much of its strength in straightening crooked material when it should be devoting its energies to producing and making the best use of the best material? Shall I be thought quite wrong in suggesting that the business of straightening crooked wood, or, to drop the figure, of correcting perversity has become almost a profession? Ah, but how difficult is the work! It has been well said, that tendencies are stronger than men; and yet how often are specific remedies sought when only constitutional renovation would be efficient? How general is the must-do-something impulse whenever an evil is detected! A desire to discover evils and a desire to correct them, ought not, of course, to incur our censure; but are not these desires through ignorance often utterly misdirected?

One of the profoundest thinkers of the present generation has called attention to the fact that we always find among people, in proportion as they are ignorant, a belief in specifics and a confidence in pressing the adoption of them. The Bushman believes that every death is occasioned by a witch, and that when the witch is killed, a countless number of deaths is prevented. But a belief in specifics is not confined to the heart of Africa. It prevails in Europe and America as well.

In Austria a great evil was thought to be the number of improvident marriages. When the Concordat made improvident marriages impossible, the reformers said: The evil is corrected. But straightway it was found that the principal result of the change was to increase enormously the number of illegitimate children: and when, to mitigate the misery of the foundlings, the government provided hospitals, the result again was to increase greatly the number of infants abandoned.

In England the Building Act was passed in answer to a demand that something should be done to prevent the overcrowding of small houses and tenements. This Act together with the Lodging-House Act accomplished its purpose; but it drove the vagrants into the streets and compelled them to sleep under bridges, or in the parks, or even, for warmth's sake, on the dunghills. It was confidently thought by Mr. Bradlaugh and others that the deplorable condition of the English peasantry, could be relieved by the formation of Leagues and Unions and the organization of strikes, but Mr. Brassey, in his book on Work and Wages, has conclusively shown that the influence of agitation among the laborers has been to frighten capital and to withdraw it from the active industries of agriculture and manufacture, and to place it in foreign bonds;—thus in fact lowering the price of labor by just so much as it has diminished the industrial pursuits. In France, during much of this century a belief in the omnipotence of specific remedies has been almost universal. Many of the people believed in the existence of a universal panacea for all their political ills, if only they could contrive to find it. In the time of the Revolution, Saint-Just declared that all the evils under which the country labored were caused by an abandonment of agricultural life; and his remedy, seriously proposed, was that all the people should be made to become farmers, and that the condition of voting should be the raising of four sheep per annum. A little later Fourier invented another method of curing the national ills; and demonstrated, apparently to the satisfaction of a large number of followers, that, if *his* mode of organizing society could only be generally adopted, "Zebras would soon come to be as much used as horses, men would live three or four hundred years instead of seventy, and, what would be still better, the globe would soon have thirty-seven millions of poets equal to Homer, thirty-seven millions of philosophers equal to Newton, and thirty-seven millions of dramatists equal to Molière."

In Wisconsin the mass of the people believed that by controlling the price of freight irrespectively of charter obligations an immense advantage would be gained by the farmers, and therefore in spite of the warnings of all political economists the "Potter Law" was passed. The result was that feeble railroads were stopped, even the stronger ones could not negotiate a bond in England or elsewhere, cons ruction ceased, and a subsequent Legislature had to hasten to repeal the law; but it was not until hundreds of thousands of dollars had been sacrificed.

In the time of the civil war men were perplexed to know how to keep down the premium on gold, as though the premium could be kept down, while millions of irredeemable paper were issuing monthly from the press and were called money. Congress even, as it will be remembered, took the matter in hand, and like the English King, commanded the tide to retire; but the only effect was to increase the violence of the mocking surges, and Congress itself had to withdraw.

Perhaps I might say that the same reformatory spirit grappled with the tremendous evil of intemperance. Societies were formed for the purpose of combating it. The evil, prodigious of itself, by the natural accumulation of zeal, came to be greatly magnified. The impression began to prevail that intemperance was enormously increasing, and that, too, in face of the fact that but a few generations ago sobriety was the exception, and that even so late as the days of our great grand-fathers the man who had never been intoxicated was a rarity. Let us abolish intoxication altogether, cried men. Let us simply make intoxication impossible by prohibiting the manufacture and sale of all that can intoxicate. The cry carried the day; with what result we all know. Alas! in spite of all law, and all officers of the law, intemperance continued, and it is even now a question whether in one single state the evil has been diminished by prohibition. Whatever may be the answer to this question, it is certain that prohibitory laws are everywhere failing, and that men are everywhere beginning to realize that the appetite for strong drink is the most energetic and persistent perversity of human nature,—has been certainly since the days of Noah, and will be probably until the milennium.

So in regard to the matter of pure administration of government. We cry out for honest men at the head of our government, and we do well. God forbid that I should say aught against such a demand. But, my friends, let us not be deluded into the belief that honesty can work miracles. Ever since the days of President Jackson, there has been lurking in our political system a poison, now torpid, now active, but ever increasing in virulence until at the present time it has permeated to the utmost extremity of the body politic. To put honest men in office so long as the virus is still working in the system, is merely to apply soothing and palliating lotions. It is well so far as it goes, but it goes only a little way. So long as there are forty thousand and more civil offices in the United States, subject to the irresponsible will of the chief magistrate, and so long as the maxim "to the victor belong the spoils" is practically in full force, there can be no assurance that government will be pure. England has passed through every stage of an experience not essentially unlike that to which we are now subjected, and it was not until the nation adopted a system of thorough civil reform that the era of pure administration was inaugurated. It is not for us to hope for a return of administrative purity until we are ourselves willing to profit by the examples of other nations. We have to return to our fathers' methods, if we would have our fathers' pure government return to us.

The greatest man of modern science said that he knew not how it might seem to others, but that it seemed to himself that he had merely walked upon the shores of time gathering here and there doubtfully a pebble, while the great world of science lay beyond his knowledge. This was the declaration of a true sage,—of a man whose judgment in all matters to which he gave his attention was scarcely inferior to his genius. The nineteenth century has inherited the fruits of Sir Isaac Newton's genius, but I fear it can hardly claim to have inherited his spirit. The American who has not yet made up his mind on every question of the day is almost a curiosity, and a genuine wonder is the man who reserves his judgment until he has completed his thinking.

It became a legal maxim as early as the days of Tacitus that the more corrupt the state the more numerous the laws—*corruptissima republica, plurimae leges,*—and yet every winter spreads thousands of laws upon our statute books, so crudely framed and so ill digested, that no inconsiderable portion of the work of the next winter is to undo them. The pregnant words with which Pliny describes the young Italy of his generation, seem almost to have been written for the young America of ours :— *Statim sapiunt, statim sciunt omnia, neminem verentur, imitantur neminem, atque ipsi sibi exempla sunt.*

Now if these tendencies and habits, of which I have spoken somewhat at length, are evils, and I think you will all concede them to be such, how are they to be successfully combated? Surely not by the application of any such mere "specific" as those to which I have alluded. The first thing to be done is to acquire a complete understanding of the nature of the difficulty to be removed or remedied. It must be understood first of all that in the vast majority of instances, the evils, both political and social, which confront us, are not diseases, but are mere signs of diseases, not accidental effects, but inevitable results, of the habit of thought and the material condition of society. The history of the race unquestionably teaches this fact with the most unmistakable distinctness—and I would that it were emblazoned upon every university and indeed upon every church—a fact well formulated by Lecky, that "the beliefs and the habits of a given age or people are mainly determined, not by specific and assignable reasons and arguments and actions, but by the general intellectual conditions of society,—conditions which cannot be suddenly created, but which can only be slowly brought about and materially changed by the combined influence of all the forces of civilization." This, if I have not read history in vain, is one of its most important lessons. If it be true, as Emerson has said, that every man is a quotation from all his ancestors, it is no less true that every nation is a quotation from all its antecedents. And yet in the very face of this lesson men expect republics built on the traditions and habits of despotism to flourish, and await miraculous changes as the result of their impotent legislation on some of the most fixed relations of society. Let us not hope that anything can effect a change in this respect excepting that more enlightened public opinion which comes from a more thorough and comprehensive knowledge of the history and experience of mankind.

And for effecting this change the hope of the country is in its higher education. Lord Bacon affirmed that "a knowledge of the speculative opinions of the men between twenty and thirty years of age, is the great source of political prophecy." The great source of political prophecy,—ah then, of what consumate importance is it, that our young men between twenty and thirty should think aright! If the saying of Lord Bacon is true,—and who can gainsay it?—the hope of our country is not solely, not even chiefly in our common schools, but largely in our colleges and universities. In every country truly free it is, after all, the cultivated mind, that is the controlling influence and motor of affairs. Its operation may not be obvious, we may not see it, we may not feel it, we may not weigh it, but like one of the forces of nature, though it works silently, its potent influence is everywhere present. The force of gravity is so gentle that we can scarcely perceive it; and yet its millions of gossamer threads bind the earth together and even keep the planets in their places.

Such is the influence of cultivated mind on society. Though Martin Luther began by begging his bread for a "pious canticle" in the streets of Eisenach, and though he was opposed by the opinions and the corruptions of his time; yet, by his studious toil of days and nights, he became able, as Lord Bacon said of him, "to summon all learning and all antiquity to his succor," and hence "was not only sustained by conquering armies and countenanced by princes, but, what was a thousand times better, was revered as a benefactor and a spiritual parent by millions of his grateful countrymen." I hold it to be the *duty*,—I do not hesitate to use the strong old Saxon word,—the *duty*, of every educator and of every seminary of higher learning to do what it can to modify the material tendencies of the age both by precept and by example. I am persuaded that what the age needs, and what our nation is sighing for, is not so much a wider diffusion of the ability to read and write, as a higher standard of excellence in morals, and in intelligence, and in learning, on the part of that class which creates, and inspires, and controls public opinion. A little learning may be better than no learning, but we must not forget that it becomes the "dangerous thing" of the proverb, when it only enables its possessor to lift himself into places of responsibility and power. Better lawyers, better physicians, better clergymen, better editors, better teachers, better legislators—these are the need of the republic, and it is only by producing these that we can make it certain that the republic will be better directed.

Within the past ten years the world has seen unrolled before its astonished vision a political panorama of most extraordinary and surprising interest; and yet how many have thought that it is chiefly remarkable, as an example of the value of higher education upon national prosperity? At the beginning of the century Prussia was torn, bleeding, impoverished, stripped of half her territory, by a foreign foe, and crushed under the cruel heel of a feudal nobility at home. But this feeble nationality fell under the immediate and the dominant influence of a great man and a great idea. The great thought of the Freiherr von Stein was, that, if Prussia ever could be built up into a strong nationality, it would be, not by devoting the chief energies of the country to the development of material resources, but to the development of men. And the whole nation was inspired with the idea, that whatever they might want a man for, the way to make the most of him, and get the most out of him for the nation, was by giving him the most thorough general training, and then the most thorough technical training. Royalty vacated its palaces at Berlin and at Bonn and universities were installed in its place. The dominant idea of the nation became this, that for every vocation in life, men must receive the best training which the nation could afford.

And we of this decade have seen the result. The little nation of two generations ago has not only become in higher learning the educator of the world, but has become the strongest power of Europe. When put to the test, its generals could plan a campaign which for comprehensiveness and unfailing certainty of result exceeded everything done under the great Napoleon, and the soldiers, after defeating the proudest legions of the world, could recreate themselves by writing and singing the *Kutschke Lied* in thirty-two languages.

I hope I shall be pardoned for speaking a single word in conclusion to those who are about to graduate. The pride of a university is her children. The great work of a university in influencing public opinion is chiefly through those whom she sends out with her honors. Do not, I charge you, do not go out with the impression that your education is completed.

The young man who goes out from a university and straightway throws aside his books is unworthy ever to have been within a university. Remember, moreover, that the life of a scholar is a life of prodigious work. The Bishop of Exeter once said, and probably said truly, that of all work of permanent value, nine tenths is drudgery. A generation ago when Mr. Choate was recognized as the great light of the American bar, the impression was rife that his genius was so colossal that he had but to stand upon his feet and perhaps with his long fingers shake up his tangled locks, in order to produce an oration that would carry sure conviction to an audience or a jury. But after his death it was revealed that no lawyer of his time prepared his cases with so minute care, and, what is of still greater interest, that during the most busy portion of his professional career, it was his rule to get at least an hour every day—rescued from sleep or society or recreation, for Latin or Greek or some other favorite study. Mr. Gowans wrote to the New York Times, that Mr. Choate, some ten years before his death, unexpectedly detained a day in New York, came into his store about ten o'clock in the morning and enquired for the department of the classics. On being directed to them the great lawyer began his researches and so eager was he, that Mr. Gowans had to interupt him in order to close the store at seven in the evening. Thus for nine hours Choate with neither food nor drink had pored over his work; and when asked what he had found, responded that he had been greatly excited over several Greek books that he had never read, and especially over a seven volume edition of the famous commentary on Homer by the Greek bishop Eustathius of the twelfth century. This was the scholarship of the man who was popularly supposed to convince juries by a kind of inspiration.

When the old man eloquent, whose culture was the consummate fruit of that earlier school of training of which I have spoken, was in the presidential chair, he "found time amidst the incessant calls and interruptions of his office to address a series of letters to his youngest son—some of them written in the busiest portion of the session—containing an elaborate analysis of the orations of Cicero, designed to aid the young man in the perusal of this, his favorite author. Some of these letters," Mr. Everett declares, "would be thought a good day's work for a scholar by profession;" and yet, at the close of one of them, he adds that he is reading Evelyn's Sylva with great delight.

The greatest lawyer of antiquity boasted that his philosophical studies had never interfered with his services to his clients and to the republic, and that he had only dedicated to them the hours which others give to their walks, their repasts and their pleasures. Looking on those voluminous works which have been the delight of all subsequent time, we cannot but be surprised at the observation. But the very fact that his philosophical works bear the names of the different villas he possessed, indicates that he composed them as the recreation of their respective retirements. They were all the result of that magic art in the employment of our leisure, which is said to multiply our days.

Thus it is that the exhortation of Goethe,—

Wie das Gestirn
Ohne Hast, aber ohne Rast,
Drehe sich jeder um die eigene Last,—

unhasting but unresting as the stars,—is the condition and the accompaniment of every great excellence. Be assured then, gentlemen, that no mere longings and sighings for the rewards of greatness will bring either greatness or its rewards. Only after a life of earnest, and honest, and persistent striving may it be said of you:—

For country and humanity he wrought,
And, which is best and happiest yet, all this
With God not parted from him—
But favoring and assisting to the end.

www.ingramcontent.com/pod-product-compliance
Lightning Source LLC
LaVergne TN
LVHW011139110826
845150LV00008B/2419

* 9 7 8 1 4 1 8 1 9 3 0 2 7 *